ONE HUNDRED DAYS

ONE HUNDRED DAYS

a blessing, a curse

poems

Adele Slaughter

Oh Girl Books 2020

Copyright © 2020 by Adele Slaughter
First American Printing
All rights reserved.
Published in 2020 by Oh Girl Books,
Los Angeles, CA 91604

No part of this book may be reproduced in any form or by any electronic or mechanical means including information storage and retrieval systems without permission in writing from the publisher, except by a reviewer.

Library of Congress Cataloguing-in-Publication Data
Slaughter, Adele, 1953
One Hundred Good Days: a blessing, a curse
poems by Adele Slaughter

ISBN: 978-X-XX-XXXXXX-X : $18.00

Acknowledgment is made to the editors of the following magazines in which these poems first appeared poetrybay.com, I told my friend and The 30/30 Project - Tupelo Press: *Is it best to line up all the bottles; I'm stuck in this story; I wonder; I've breathed a garden for you; A still life; I am a gale; We live in reverse; Living; To become a hero.*

Special thanks to Arran Russell for his cover design,
and Mark E. Cull for the book design and layout.

Grateful thanks to Diana Charkalis for reading and re-reading
and to Sanora Bartels for always believing in me.

for Jeff Kober

Contents

Preface . . . 11

WINTER

1. Is it best to line up all the bottles by size, . . . 17
2. A virus tight in my chest, . . . 18
3. The last two numbers reverse, . . . 19
4. Stuck in this story, . . . 20
5. All night the moon—Wolf Moon . . . 21
6. I wonder . . . 22
7. We fall . . . 23
8. Why is forgiveness . . . 24
9. Inside your fractured brain . . . 25
10. What is remembered has already changed. . . . 26
11. Going through old boxes, . . . 27
12. I've breathed a garden for you . . . 28
13. You are still. . . . 29
14. The smell of dry-roasted beans . . . 30
15. After a chance encounter with a former flame: . . . 31
16. I see chalked graffiti on a wall in Le Marais. . . . 32
17. What are gargoyles but fancy gutters spitting . . . 33
18. Yesterday it poured. . . . 34
19. I love you even when I'm alone. . . . 35
20. A few feet above ground, . . . 36
21. I told my friend, . . . 37
22. Apricot kernels, once thought a bitter almond, . . . 38
23. My brother, creature of myth, . . . 39
24. Age changes memory . . . 40
25. Memory is a bag of glass. . . . 41

SPRING

26.	Stone path,	45
27.	Tufts of poppy feathery petals	46
28.	Imagine getting	47
29.	My childhood brick house stands,	48
30.	The moon woke me.	49
31.	Waiting for that windfall to live.	50
32.	I hacked a bougainvillea	51
33.	I grasp the woody stalk of a lilac shrub,	52
34.	This week I've broken two bowls, a cobalt plate	53
35.	A piece of turquoise sea-glass,	54
36.	I am lagging behind.	55
37.	If there is something good	56
38.	There are creatures in the natural world that	57
39.	Strands of her red hair	58
40.	There is a lake	59
41.	I heard that many people in comas are awake.	60
42.	In a Montana store,	61
43.	On the side of a Park City road,	62
44.	The maples stretch this morning.	63
45.	Flying buttresses muster support for archways,	64
46.	. . . easier to lift a fallen branch off the road,	65
47.	A still life	66
48.	I am a gale,	67
49.	We live in reverse.	68
50.	Each time the heart breaks	69

SUMMER

51.	Living through words,	73
52.	At the screen door,	74
53.	New York wind lifts girls' dresses,	75
54.	Wandering the halls of the Met	76
55.	Driving through Central Park,	77
56.	He lingers—	78
57.	Plums you pick up from the ground—	79
58.	Ptolemy imagined everything moved 'round	80
59.	Growth rings inside a tree,	81
60.	Leave the porch light on.	82
61.	Unencumbered sleep	83
62.	Riding my bicycle to town,	84
63.	In heavy summer air, children count down in a	85
64.	As plates shift underground,	86
65.	Roosting in eucalyptus,	87
66.	Damn it.	88
67.	There is no-thing so small	89
68.	In the fall the air was cool,	90
69.	I would like to speak about birch trees	91
70.	Take in the drive up the coast.	92
71.	Clang, ca-clang.	93
72.	You are	94
73.	I am washing the dishes again.	95
74.	I held a needle,	96
75.	No longer married,	97

FALL

76.	Today my nose sprouted red.	101
77.	Every city has a melody.	102
78.	We honor the dead with	103
79.	"I am Diego." That is true.	104
80.	"I am Frida."	105
81.	When I married	106
82.	Eyes closed, meditating,	107
83.	The first mistake, a gentle nudge.	108
84.	Picking at a shard of wood	109
85.	I'm hot and scratchy,	110
86.	At the door of the local coffee shop:	111
87.	Pine needles form arrows shooting at	112
88.	In a fuzzy memory	113
89.	Define intimacy:	114
90.	A sable brush spreads	115
91.	Yesterday	116
92.	Living—	117
93.	To become a hero:	118
94.	Most nights are too long—	119
95.	The night is starless,	120
96.	There is a heaviness	121
97.	Dark circles around my hazel irises.	122
98.	Before the darkness settled in,	123
99.	We live in the darkness of time. Some say it's a	124
100.	When it comes time	125

Preface

A few years ago I wrote a poem a day for 365 consecutive days. Sometime later I wrote a poem a day for a month for The 30/30 Project for Tupelo Press. Writing a poem day by day was at times challenging, finding a spark each day to inspire me and then expressing that inspiration in images and words. For me, the greatest gift of this was finding the transformational in the mundane. It became a spiritual practice, waking me to the moments of my life with the express intention of sharing the essence I could find there—in the quiet moments of contemplation, in the triggering of childhood memories, or in the spaces of darkness and separation that are a part of any life. These poems became a pathway back to the version of me that I cherish, and that I trust will be recognized by those I love as the truth of me.

This search for truth of experience, I believe, is a part of being human. When we engage in this pursuit we connect with each other in ways that uplift both speaker and listener; and when we connect, it helps us see past the seeming differences of politics and opinion. Perhaps these poems might inspire others to see the beauty in themselves and those around them, in places generally overlooked or ignored.

I always have identified with Emily Dickinson—not because my poetry was like hers, but because she wrote in isclation; as if no one possibly could care about poetry, other than the poet herself.

I recently discovered that Dickinson herself wrote a poem a day in the years 1862 and 1863. And there are other examples of poets who wrote a daily poem for a year, wonderful poets including Robert Bly, William Stafford, Frank O'Hara, James Schuyler, Ted Berrigan, Joe Brainard, A. R. Ammons and David Lehman. I'm sure there are more. Perhaps they knew one of the things I learned in my own process, that poetry lives in the everyday, in the simplest of moments, and that sometimes those moments can lead to the most profound of personal insights.

I also found that writing a poem a day brought compassion into my world. The daily challenge to find meaning and happiness in my life became easier, supported by this practice of examination and recontexualization of things is the work of the poet. I have heard that how we do anything is how we do everything, and this seeking of the poetic in the everyday was a great gift I gave myself.

These 100 poems, numbered, not titled, are chosen from the daily practice and represent the essence of that process. They are divided into four sections, representing the four seasons.

I see this book as being a conversation between myself and the something greater that lies hidden in all things. My hope is that it might offer you the reader some small version of that experience.

Adele Slaughter, 2020

ONE HUNDRED DAYS

WINTER

1

Is it best to line up all the bottles by size, large to small—
or let them sit on the shelf in whatever sequence you set them down?

There's no answer to the question, really,
but it's easier to find objects when everything has a place.

Time creates a widening circle of disorder
and we lose more every day.

The list is endless:
glasses, keys, courage, heart, weight, lovers.

It seems harder and harder to let go.
Still,
like it or not we are becoming weightless.
Either we
release what has been taken,
or fill our pockets with the things that will drown us.

2
After Pablo Neruda

A virus tight in my chest,
poetry won't leave me.
I cough up words
odd birds that insist on
chirping outside my window.
One strikes the glass pane,
I pick up the stunned creature,
cradle it 'til it can fly.
A blessing, a curse,
the verse in my ears,
tangle in my hair,
get lost in the laundry.
Words I try to get rid of
like a broken umbrella.
She finds her way
down the cracked chimney,
through rat holes,
as sunlight on a wall.
She does not care.
Poetry does not care.
Caught in my hands,
caught in my throat,
caught in my heart.
Until she's gone again.

3

The last two numbers reverse,
making the deposit wrong.
Silence is loud,
north is south.
I live in the breech position.
Flowers unfurl in my hand.
Waves return to the shore.
I stop getting lost
when I surrender
my original cartographer.

4

Stuck in this story,
at the beginning...
until I can remember
a leaf on the sidewalk.
Sunlight on lavender;
Meyer lemons on supple branches,
parrots in palm trees.

He can see through parrot eyes too.
The bay reflects turquoise.

He doesn't care what story He's tuned into.
The young girl talks to a ladybug on her arm,
a mother pulls her children from a burning car.

He whispers in my ear "surrender."
But I hear "don't blunder."
I think I have failed.
He keeps laughing.
Although this offends me,
maybe He's on to something.

5

All night the moon—Wolf Moon
achingly full
hangs in a pale grey sky—
illuminates our sleeping bodies.
Your breath heavy, deep like a cavern.
I wake easily.
We glow in the dark.
Our house and the two of us;
blue embers of loneliness.

6

I wonder
how you love me
in spite of annoying habits.

I admit it—I don't screw
lids on jars.
You shake a bottle,
salad dressing
coats the kitchen wall.

It's a family trait—
alcoholism
or clogged arteries—
not screwing lids on.

As sorry as I am,
I hate admitting I'm wrong.

You laugh—you hate it too.

I say, let it go, I was born,
make mistakes . . .
grateful you love me
anyway.

7

We fall
together in anger
in fits and starts,
like sacked potatoes,
bouncing at odds.

We burn
until
ash residue
rises on drafts,
scatters
messy cinders.

We gather up
fistfuls of powdered remains.
Settle down.
Reabsorbed.

8

Why is forgiveness
so difficult
when a hummingbird
can beat his wings
90 times per second,
fly backward,
and drink nectar from honeysuckle.
Shouldn't it be easy
to say sorry,
I didn't mean to hurt you.

9

Inside your fractured brain
    you were a painter
dreaming of landscapes and Paris.

They stuffed you into a mathematician
    painting numbers, counting beds.

You fed me liver, I swallowed it whole
    before I knew it was overcooked
and she burnt the Brussel sprouts beyond eating.

Butterscotch candies sweetened my breath.
Yanked to my feet, bow legged, I stumbled.

Chewing on a rubber fish in my playpen.
    Black and white photos with scalloped edges.

My tongue lolled in my mouth
Like a parrot, squawking the words
    You taught me to say
Pretty girl, pretty girl
    Good girl.

10

What is remembered has already changed.
Each time I describe a moment, a detail shifts.
Wading into a cold stream toes freeze.
At bedtime mother reads Uncle Wiggly to us—
all five girls wearing pajamas with feet, reciting:
Now I lay me down to sleep
I pray the Lord my soul to keep . . .

Memories seem untouched,
but they're not.
Daffodils, mustard collars frilled,
bending toward the table like new.
The grace of firsts—
when I saw myself in his hazel eyes.
That kiss beside the cherry-red car.

I meet him standing at the ocean's edge.
Offer him a blue-black rock.
He takes it as if he has never held such a stone.
Makes a mobile with sea-glass and driftwood,
hangs in the yard.
It dazzles, dances, hums
reminds me of no other thing.

11

Going through old boxes,
my hands are full

of the dust
I no longer need.

12

I've breathed a garden for you
bent over the plants,
weeding and pruning helps them thrive.
Different shades
reach through the dirt,
fingers weaving together in prayer.

A sudden frost stiffens the grass.
The agave, struck with leaf burn,
look weary and stung with surprise,
scolded while minding their own business.

Can you imagine my ache
at their early death?
Come spring I will
speak to them gently, coaxing abundance.
Unsure I can mend the harsh words.
Wish I could unsay them.

13

You are still,
your voice low,
steady hands.
I like you this way.
You, a star
shooting quietly without fanfare
lighting the way.
Tracks of snails
glisten on the sidewalk.

14

We are what we think.
All that we are arises with our thoughts.
With our thoughts, we make the world.
        —Buddha

The smell of dry-roasted beans
strong, better than coffee itself.
Radiance shoots through the mist of your body—
making pinholes into parallel
worlds.

A season of mockingbirds and butterflies
soar, alight on the broadleaf
of the lion's tail, orange in the flower bed.
Here for a moment. Gone.
You glisten.

If it's all made up—
why not ecstasy.

15

After a chance encounter with a former flame:
we drink a demitasse,
you talk until your voice trembles
and your fingers become still.
Your passion folds into an origami swan.
Let it take flight,
it's better than stopping.
A second espresso.

We stroll, arms linked, to the great Cathedral,
where gargoyles are angels.
Color comes back to your cheeks.
Be kind.

I see you straining,
frozen in marble.
You're lion weary, mossy.

I scream at the moon,
rising and setting every day,
the luxury of movement.
Free to leave.

16

I see chalked graffiti on a wall in Le Marais.
Lack of Content Is the Message
I point-smile at the homonym.
Walking on stones to the church on the hill—
the mountain of the martyr—Montmartre.
A decapitated saint once strolled the city.
He held his head in his arms,
the way I am beside myself.
There is the me you see and the me I imagine myself to be.

Meditating in the French mass,
it might seem as if I'm sleeping.
Amens float through me,
as laundry-line sheets.
Divine hands pin up prayers.
I stroll along the bumpy rues,
rough boys jump the turnstile—
holy shit—water splashes.
My biggest fear—
to turn away from myself.

17

What are gargoyles but fancy gutters spitting water
from carefully carved facades.
We ask them to protect cathedrals. And they do.
They are our desire to snap and snarl
What we long to accept.
Our deepest fears as tiny monsters.
Standing in the dome of Sacre Coeur,
I found mine—
screaming bloody murder, afraid of heights.
What ineffectual creatures
powerless to climb down the winding staircase and go home.

18

Yesterday it poured.
An earthworm lifted its pink mouth

from a puddle on the side-
walk searching for land higher up.

Puddles make it safe to crawl
and shed what we rely on.

19

I love you even when I'm alone.
A hawk circles above
glides on currents
sated, regal, he
covers the sun. I see his red tail—
his full belly—his calm dreaming
stirs the dreamer in me
wind on my cheeks, warmth on my shoulders.
Drifting on warm gusts.
There is no elevation higher.
There is no dream sweeter
in this moment as I inhale
and dip close to the earth.

20

A few feet above ground,
barn swallows search for insects.
Mud nests in crooks of bridges.

They dive into naked sky.
Cliff-jumpers
laughing all the way down.

No one's going to arrest swallows,
clap them in handcuffs.
Not even the mountains.

They float in quiet ease.
If God can't catch them
nobody can.

21

I told my friend,
Your God is a miser,
stingy with a black heart,
wrinkled like a raisin
no, even a dried fruit is too plump.
His chest is hard coal.
It's the way we were raised—
pulled up from our boot straps
spanked, shoved against a wall.
I get it . . . I get it.
It's why I can take so much,
but my patience has snapped,
a belt cracking on my back.
I can take it, but don't want to.

No one really believes we were set
on this world only to be told
you're not worthy,
and yet this is what we tell our selves
inside our chests,
small beats
hardening.

22

> *Count the almonds . . .*
> *Make me bitter.*
> *Count me among the almonds.*
> —Paul Celan

Apricot kernels, once thought a bitter almond,
have just enough poison to heal.
A waitress friend in the late 1970s
diagnosed with uterine cancer
swore she healed herself eating three apricot kernels a day.
Stopped eating sugar.
Her doctors couldn't explain it.
Her womb was clear.

These days I open the front door to feed our feral cat
and a cricket leaps from under the doormat, quick—smiling.

In the backyard squirrels tear oranges to bits,
my slender dog sucks juice from fallen fruit,
orange trees bloom—a carpet of snowy blossoms.

Maybe it isn't the tiny bits of seeds or cyanide that heals,
but how we step into our lives believing in the power
of nature to heal itself—sure-footed.
Calling in the silence beneath the static.

23

My brother, creature of myth,
offered a message.

Loki, a trickster god—
terrified us by the campfire.
telling stories of a talking fly
trapped in a matchbox.
His flames erased my shadows.

He made a map of me:
how to fall from a height and roll,
how to fight,
how to not get hurt,
how to be brave at father's rage,
how to let him cradle me.

How could he, this clown-angel
with a damaged wing
get to me?
Someone whose clumsiness healed me
in what I needed most.

24

Age changes memory
the same way the patina of an oak bookcase
alters through wear.
It's not the thing-itself.

I am still riding toward my brother
the way Dad took us to the farm for the first time.
Hauling ass in the yellow pick-up, the windows cracked.
My lips full, my knees pulled into my chest.
The truck straining up the hills,
breezing through cut shale.

This bouncy truck carries with it:
the times we got hit, climbing trees,
riding bareback under a full moon,
him urging me to throw a punch, his broken nose.
What I have not been willing to lose: him.
Not his gold hair or devil-may-care.

Awake or asleep I am
barefoot on the gravel driveway, our lies,
the unspoken, what we never could have known.
A drifter riding rails, a prisoner to motion.

25

Memory is a bag of glass.
I try
to pull apart the suffering,
pick off the smashed pieces,
a label from a wine bottle
holds bits together.
Instead of picking it up,
I throw the bag away.
There's no salvaging
sharp and sticky.

SPRING

26

Stone path,
a blanket of thyme in the cracks.
Overhead, hacking blackbirds,
dumb as my pitiless thumb.
The warm beginning of spring, breezy—
sprouted poppy seeds I planted,
promise a crop of wafer flowers,
offering communion.
A season of maybes.
Grasses wave
as if to say
begin again.

27

Tufts of poppy feathery petals
were trampled today by my husband.
I sobbed
at their innocence.
Naïve shoes flattened their heads.
It embarrasses me to weep about shredded poppies,
but then that is me
torn apart by missteps.

28

Imagine getting
a different license.
Drive down a street with a new name.
My deliverance from . . .
I remind myself
the angel watching the ocean is me.
My son visits,
plays the guitar, whistles in my study.
The poppies revive.
A rhythm
of their own.
Swirling tunes.
Sleeping son.
No need to be anyone else.

29

My childhood brick house stands,
creaking willows define the dried-up pond.
Dandelions splinter, spores take flight.
Cadmium tulips break soil
reminding me of a primrose path; overgrown.
A family once lived here, six kids
calling red light, green light.
A long-legged girl in the yard
caught fireflies,
studied how they sputter.
She trailed luminescence at dusk.

30

The moon woke me.
Shadow bright,
it was day at night.
I can't recall who I am without You.
You, who tell me my name.
You, who whisper in my ear.
You, to whom I chant
come home, come home,
rest now, tomorrow is green.

31

Waiting for that windfall to live.
I ask myself,
why not do it now?
Winnings already here:

in the clouds gathering, the fog rolling in,
the wet streets, the one you love pumping gas,
the duck's smooth landing on the river.

Having enough is its own grace.
Remember the ancient couple who
gave a stranger their last bit of food
and got a magic pitcher, with limitless milk?

Handfuls of kindness.

32

I hacked a bougainvillea
that blocked our entryway,
from between flagstones.
Thorny branches growing pell-mell
scratched my arms,
the roots, rotting
wormwood,
unearthed the bitterness in my garden.

33

I grasp the woody stalk of a lilac shrub,
star-like flowers brush my nose.
I inhale the four-lobed lavender.

In a flash, I'm on grandma's stone porch,
run and hide beneath the Concord grape arbor,
staining fingers and tongue with purple juice.

Here, scent came alive.
Toast she made at dawn,
her face lotion, the musty couch cushions,

wood smoke in the house.
Wisps linger like errant hairs.
All of this happening at once.

34

This week I've broken two bowls, a cobalt plate
and a glass with fishes swimming in a circle.
Shattered dishes are piling up,
shards pour out the windows.
Cut fingers bleed, sweeping up
the pieces of what's left
so I won't step on the slivers.

When I was a kid
whatever I picked up
slipped from my grasp,
unbidden.
I chipped myself
bit by bit.

You ask me how I am—
some other girl answers: fine.
The one you see before you is a hologram.
Behind her is a cracked madwoman.
I ask her to stop picking up,
but she just keeps cleaning and cleaning.

35

A piece of turquoise sea-glass,
sharp edges rubbed smooth,
lit from inside,
from all that tumbling
through surf, salt, sand.
No danger of cutting.
Hold it, let it glow.

36

I am lagging behind.
I used to run to keep up,
now I amble.
Let the dishes build up.

37

If there is something good
Let it happen now—
Bursting, swift, cascading.
I'm ready to grab it,
maybe for the first time
ever.
I open my arms,
urge the weight
to roll in.

38

There are creatures in the natural world that glow.
Deep-sea anglerfish
in the depths
or nocturnal larvae, railroad worms,
or fungi on the composting leaves in the woods.
Blue-green glistening threads
chart our bleak forests.
My favorite, the firefly, lightning bug.
flying beetles sparkle at dusk with yellow-green tails
to attract a mate.
Light adapts to darkness—
it's what we do.
Sunflowers and orchids bend toward the sun.
In a season of eclipse, we are light.

39

Strands of her red hair
caught in a hairbrush lift
up and down; a chest heaving.
When she said goodbye,
she called my name,
adding a term of endearment—
"my sweet."
Her aroma lingers on the pillow,
suds melt into the wood floors she scrubbed.
I ask myself, did I love her enough?
Did I tell her what she meant?

40

There is a lake
where geese flicker on the surface,
loons laugh—scary, comforting, across the way.
An afternoon of blowsy promise—
a sail fills, urging the boat forward.
The main sheet ripples in the breeze.
The boat cuts a deep curved wake,
hums an even tune, not much variation—
a kind of om, the keel vibrating.
You tell me, *this is only a dream*.
I smile gently, say, *no* . . .

I have spent a day on
a sailboat, letting the sun bake my legs.
I've watched the sail unfurl,
the skiff skimming the water.
And no one woke me.

I am awake.

41

I heard that many people in comas are awake.
Unable to respond, except for a tiny tear
or a trembling lip or one finger flickering.
Still alive. We call them vegetables.

No one is listening:
men on death row
who profess their innocence,
or sane people in a locked ward,
pleading for release.

Studies show the comatose are happy.
They see themselves playing tennis,
gathering sea shells,
sitting in a chaise with suntanned legs reading a good book.
Brain waves
of those imagining compared to those in action
aren't any different.

Often we leave them for dead.
Let's bathe them, stroke their heads,
speak to them gently.
Wake up.

42

In a Montana store,
hundreds of yellow peeping chicks
huddle under warming lights.

Visiting the farmhouse in disrepair,
tulips, lilacs and climbing roses
smothered by weeds.
Gardens overrun with
foxtails and burrs.
Piles of used tires abandoned in the field.
Mold on roofs—
the blacksmith shop and chicken coop collapsing
from the weight of rain and snow.
Claw into the slaughterhouse—empty.
Damp root cellar,
once filled with apples from the orchard
too wet to store anything.
The bunkhouse for field hands filled with sprung
box springs and empty beer bottles.

We won't bring chicks home to lay eggs.
There are no more
horses and cattle in the faded barn.
No sugar beets.

We watch the dogs chase after the geese that stop by
on their way to Canada,
honking, calling to us from their V-formation as they shift.
Reminding us we have a place in the order of things.

43

On the side of a Park City road,
a baby deer
hit by a car, bleeding,
not dead, barely here.

Last summer
I came upon a snapping turtle
hit and wounded.
Pulled the turtle off the road,
called Animal Control, who told me
there's no money to rescue wounded animals.

I know there's no help for this baby deer.
I want to nuzzle her,
but up close she startles me.
Wild, beyond what I know,
her breathing slows,
head yearning toward the lights of
a passing truck. She flickers.
I whisper good-bye.

44

The maples stretch this morning.
A crow, then a mourning dove
whirring, scrape the sky.
I am a balloon floating on gusts
among the yellow leaves.
Some day all this
will be
not even a
whistle.

45

Flying buttresses muster support for archways,
pushing against gravity.
On a large veranda, marble floors.
Potted ferns.
Hot winds blow across a lawn,
heat bakes roses to black beauty.
A flash rain floods the streets.
Your eyes pool to emerald.
I float on you.

46

. . . easier to lift a fallen branch off the road,
easier for my feet to grow roots into the dirt,
easier to watch an acorn elaborate itself into an oak.
Easier to stand in tree-pose and hold up my hands
to prevent the earth from turning 'round the sun.
Best not to stare too hard at this.
Me loving you, you, loving me.
I could stop, I guess,
but it would be . . .

47

A still life
on our kitchen windowsill—
a tiny vase with white tulips.
On the floor, air-worn petals
thin as the skin of a young girl's wrist.
They crumble when you touch them,
mantels turned to ash.
Between sleeping and waking,
a thin membrane between here and there
shinning through—scattered slips of tulips.

48

I am a gale,
you are the ocean.

While I run along the surface of you,
you remain unmoved by my nattering.

I blow billows into clouds,
you recast their undulating shapes.

I tear branches off a tree,
you tote them downstream.

We're the same,
you lie to me.
I sense our disparity—
and long to be ocean.

49

We live in reverse.
As in a mirror, it's all flipped.
The writing backwards.

We get married.
They gut my chest to fix the beating organ.
You pull out the tubes so I can stand again

whispering it wasn't meant to be this way—
fists full of blood.
You held me—I became cotton.

We found what we both have
the ability to survive.

50

Each time the heart breaks
it shatters, expands.
A new muscle
emerges
shedding its stiff cover.
Splinters leaping
like grasshoppers
off a shaft of wheat,
scratching my strong legs as I run.

SUMMER

51

Living through words,
hidden under moss.
Images crumble and reassemble;
dust bunnies under the bed.
I scoop the ones I can.
Pen to paper.
They have their own librettos.
It's clear:
now is all we have.
Write verses,
let them speak on their own.

52

At the screen door,
the cowbell
calls you to supper.
Running in, knees dirty,
hungry for poetry.

Words in your mouth squinch,
explode,
or soak sweetly on your tongue,
blackberries picked from brambles.
Or pucker, tart lemons.
Words can link or
crumble,
separating us—
a butterfly fluttering off,
a maple seed pod skittering.

53

New York wind lifts girls' dresses,
makes tattoos dance. A hawk swirls around cornices.
Boys leap from a rock with a 50-foot drop
into the Hudson and swim to the other side,
uncover a tarnished placard commemorating
this island sold for beads and 24 bucks.

Easy to sell yourself cheap.

54
for Lucian Freud

Wandering the halls of the Met
through perfumed rooms and long corridors lined with paintings . . .
a smoky Joan, armor guarding her round breasts.

Skipping steps, turn a corner,
run into Lucian Freud.

His paintings with crinkled skin,
glinting baby blues,
fleshy oils.
The one with the sad face and grey tones.
I know her.
I am her.

Two men on a couch, naked and friendly.
Painted hips, blue veins, bodies with skins of flesh.
I love them.

A large transvestite with a huge cock,
head bowed, spilling folds of plump.
It hurts to be alive.

To be seen up close
by Freud's stark refusal
to paint us more beautiful than we are.
Our misshapen limbs.
Tender strokes smeared on canvas.

55
for a dead poet

Driving through Central Park,
You place your faux-fox cap on my head,
my hand slides along the fur,
my eyes trace your strong jaw,
your sad turquoise eyes.

Later in your Gramercy Park hotel room,
lavender shadows,
pen in hand,
slash lines of a poem:
Build bridges.
Don't make connections.
Every thought doesn't need an antecedent.

On top of covers,
you hover over me:
I could look at this face for a lifetime.
An impossible compliment.

I don't regret refused sex.
An unforgotten wakeful night.
I don't suppose even a small memory of me
occurred one time before you died—
You: more in love with romance,
Me: *a cheap Lana Turner,*
you didn't take me seriously.

I apprehend the language
of our bridge.

56

He
lingers—
a note played on the piano
resonating

a guitar string across the room.
She—a sympathetic vibration.

He whistles into the air.
A distant purr,
humming tunes.

She
writes them down.
Speaks quietly.
Prayers for the lost.

57

Plums you pick up from the ground—
warm, sweet and perfectly ripe,
you discover poems hidden in the bushes,
and pluck them—
a coin pulled from behind the ear of a child.

58

Ptolemy imagined everything moved 'round Mother Earth
holding herself still. A complicated universe.

Copernicus believed the sun was the center.
Stars were fixed points of light,
flecks of crystal in a stone.

Astronomers thought we move in circles.
But we don't.
We move in a simpler truth of wobbly arcs.

The little i as the center of the Universe
is partly correct.
All of it happening
because we lost a pair of glasses
or married the wrong man.

The nuns used to tell me God is in everyone,
my elementary mind couldn't comprehend the implications.

All of us as one jumbled, unified sweater made with divine thread
emerging from the infinite, only to return.
Knitted:
stars, Earth, pine cones, fire escapes, wind, sidewalks, bones, dirt.
Swallows chirp in the garden next to orange poppies,
Mexican heather, plum, and fig trees.

It doesn't matter what we see
or who we divorce.

The sun keeps rising.

59

Growth rings inside a tree,
Black stripes on the tail of a raccoon,
Saturn's rings: Alpha, Beta, Gamma.
A gold band on a ring finger,
the ring around a lunar eclipse.
Your family,
a hula-hoop.

The barbs are all yours.
You file the jagged edges smooth,
until nothing holds you back.
Spheres again.

60

Leave the porch light on.
Ignore the moths
crowding the bulb.
Flick away their dusty dark wings.
Illumination.

61

Unencumbered sleep
rises from a spring.
I sit and watch water bubble and drink
the clear cold dream of the Earth.

62

Riding my bicycle to town,
buying candy with spare change.
Reading under a blanket, sucking sweets.
Evenings hauling the kitchen table to the lawn,
setting it for dinner at dusk.
After dinner, the kids play Mother May I?
What I remember
is a checkered beetle in amber.

63

In heavy summer air, children count down in a game of hide-'n'-seek.
Here, a bare bulb is lit on the back porch. I hide where no one will venture.
Breathing. There is a field like the horizon, in between buzzy silvery static.
Slowly, daylight darkens. Stop my breath. No one can find me.
Still, She always knows where I am
and tells me when to breathe again.

64

As plates shift underground,
mercy
is slow.
Bit by bit
mountains move
rearranging the world's edge.

65

Roosting in eucalyptus,
crows descend on the food left for our cat.
They shriek inky opinions
to any who listen, and scour the gravel for seeds.
The yard's a heap of mussel-black birds,
pecking at what remains.

I dislike their furtive gaze,
how they lope into flight when caught off guard.

Watching them hop unevenly across the lawn,
scrounging for grubs,
I am reminded how I find fault
and hate them even more.

Just as I set my gun's sight on the big one,
he tilts his head, a blank eye stares,
crow being crow.

I fire.

66

Damn it.
A raven flew up in front of me,
glistening silent wings,
stunningly strong,
somersaulting through foliage,
feathers extending.
Spreading quills.
A judgement ripples across my mind.
I have been afraid of them so long,
almost hating
these heavy birds.

67

There is no-thing so small it won't come back to you.
The bliss of walking from the pine forest to the dock,
and setting out on the lake to ski.
Keep up your speed and you'll break through the wake,
ski on one ski, even skim on your feet alone,
hydroplaning. All the nerves start in your feet.
Spray obscures, knees bounce; shrieks of pleasure.
Climb in the boat, legs shaking.
Shiver, sit on a wet towel, watch the next skier.
It's okay to feel, you've earned it. Think of all you've let go.
When isn't this a test?
Things you knew are in the silt slowly oozing
their way back and you will get to choose
whether to scoop them up or let them sink again.

Go ahead: take a second spin.

68

In the fall the air was cool,
soil rusty-brown, loamy.
My sisters and I dug holes
and filled them with water,
holes deep and wide for roots to grow
straight down and fan out.
We worked quickly.
Best not to expose them to the air.
We packed them in, snug.
Five girls planted a forest.
Summer now,
four-hundred pines.
Roots buried.
Sturdy. Tall.

69

Birch trees rooted side by side and sway in unison,
rubbing against each other.
I have heard they whisper the secrets of the forest.
Growing as one mind,
their bark is silver parchment peeling.
Birches bend easily are fluid.
Butterflies and moths feed on them.
Even though it looks as if they might—
they'll never pull up root and walk away.
How many shooting stars
took root here in this
stand of silver birches?
Woods of white ghosts from another world.

70

Take in the drive up the coast.
Toward land: mauve mountains,
sage hills, brown dirt, high fire alert.
Toward China, a wide expanse of sea
changes the way you see.
Wind-sculpted pines line the shore.
Fields of peppers and cauliflower.
California Oak growing around a rock.
Water erodes the riverbed.
A train huffs on a track.
Pelicans dive-bomb into the waves
and disappear.

71

Clang, ca-clang.

Footsteps echo across a wood bridge
running to a school bell.
Ghosts of sheep graze.

Ten thousand rivers soak the ground.
Gravity pulls water toward itself.
Concrete holds.

We dance on the surface.
To the Earth we live as long as butterflies.
Gravity has no pull on spirit.

In June, as cherry blossoms are crushed,
we learn to disappear.

72

You are
the grooves in your brain,
neither genius nor dullard, you
are a person of some interest.
A hoary devil
gossiping about you
to your face.

You soldier on.

73

I am washing the dishes again.
No broken plates,
but they don't feel clean.

Out the window
a leaf skitters along the pavement.
Stormy gusts, crisp air,
the Santa Ana winds
stirring up trouble.

74

I held a needle,
slender between my fingers.
In a gathering of women
I was taught how to thread an eye,
tie a knot,
slip the sharp point into the cloth
assembling hems.

My mother embroidered ivory linen,
stretched in a hoop, on her lap.
She chain-stitched flowers, leaves, branches
for our dining room chairs.

In China the forbidden stitch
caused seamstresses to go blind.
When I divorced, I bought
a tiny flower stitched into black cloth.

75

No longer married,
sighted,
not sewing thread into black cloth,
or watching my mother pass evenings
with embroidery,
I hear silence.

All I hear some days.

FALL

76

Today my nose sprouted red.
A blooming rose,
blood-soaked tissue.
Head thrown back,
nose pinched,
gurgling.
A surprising stream
flowing up my spine and from my nose.
A toy soldier in uniform
and his tin drum
counting beats:
Ta tumm tat tumm ta tumm
Virgin Mary in a thicket of roses.
Five wounds of Jesus.
The fire extinguished,
leaving as quickly as it came.

77

Every city has a melody.
Think of Mexico City—an exotic girlfriend.
Her soprano reverberates into a sea of stars.
El canto de una ciudad.

We hear her in a marketplace:
silver, gemstones, paper woven bracelets, baskets,
the big wooden doors, their steel latches,
backstreets, the roads made of compressed lava.
Claro que si, she hums.

The city's song streams from *las ninas* on the streets,
orange shirted boys harmonize—
soccer players forever loved by dark girls.
Buenos dias, she says in the elevator,
cinnamon and candy bread.
Good morning to you, Mexico.

A storm erupts.
Lightning cracks open the sky,
dust and leaves—swirling tornados.
Raining rose petals
sing Mexico's song.

78

We honor the dead with
jade masks.

In underground tombs
kings sleep hiding gold ingots
in their pockets.

Spirit does not give up.
The future lives in our cells.

79

"I am Diego." That is true.
"I paint what I see." That is a lie.

Weavers, sugar workers, *campesinos*.
Upright, thick bodies
holding up a country—
their heavy haunches rooted,
their slanted eyes squint.
Behind them fields are impregnated with corn.
Fires burn in smelters,
women wear glowing halos,
the men are stars, burning.

Diego stopped making art.
Cut loaves of hearty bread,
serving soup to the poor.
"Today is split pea."
This is true.

80

"I am Frida."
"I paint self-portraits. I am so often alone."

She isolates her brittle bones,
and draws a cage encasing her torso,
a rifle becomes her spine.

Confined to a metal cot, strapped.
Pinned and folded sheets tuck
her in tightly.
Crutches, a fused skeleton,
an ashen face baring teeth.
She draws herself—
55 portraits.
In her last paintings
She is out of focus.

All that rage,
one leg severed,
Frida dimmed,
an echo of an echo,
a marionette of her own making
at her early death.

81

When I married
I drank his depression—
my morning tears ached for joy,
a slice of chocolate cake
couldn't transform it.
No sedation was enough.

My shoulder blades sprouted feathers,
my best friend died in a car crash.
I smoked to grieve.
My wings, cracked, broken,
folded in
until I could travel again.
I didn't plan this.

82

Eyes closed, meditating,
I swore the snoring was my friend
just across the meadow.
Eyes open, he was gone.
My body was snoring.

When I was three
I fell on a screwdriver, nearly poked out my eye.
My mother held me, red spreading on her white blouse,
the one with the pearl buttons.
As the doctor lowered a cloth over my eyes
to stitch me up,
I shot out of my body, across the room.
They tended a little girl in a pink dress.
I didn't know yet
she was actually me—
not firmly settled in,
not captive in her mind.

Today, the glue is wearing thin—
this mind, these emotions,
there is the vast meadow of me.

83

The first mistake, a gentle nudge.
The second a shove.
The third time's the harshest,
takes everything.
Like being thrown from a motorcycle,
lucky to be alive.
Splintered.

Unlearn the lesson now
to get the next one.
Most people pack their bags and leave.

Imagine my glee when I find you,
waiting
under the covers.

84

Picking at a shard of wood
stuck in my flesh,
I use a sharp needle
to dig an opening,
carefully hooking the splinter.
Hope the wood doesn't shred
under my skin.
I remove it whole,
enjoy the relief.
It takes a thorn to remove a thorn.
I throw them both away.

85

I'm hot and scratchy,
leafless boughs,
a wool blanket,
a sore throat.

I want to be a supernova.
I'm a drunken iris swelling—
indigo, ultra-violet, vermillion,
exploding, burning, expelling all my matter.

I travel far above this world
where oceans look
serene no matter what violence.
All storms pass—
the gas, the carbon blows away,

until I become
the Milky Way.

86

At the door of the local coffee shop:
a woman passes.
Waves of wrinkles lay
on her skin, mouth,
at her eyes crow's feet.
Some fine, some deep.
She glows,
the petal of a buttercup,
a piece of driftwood.
I sip my breath.
A face I can hold.

87

Pine needles form arrows shooting at
tumbling clouds.
After-rain clears the air
until
you blossom.

88

In a fuzzy memory
I see a black-'n-white B movie.
Female prisoners.
Male guards thrashing women,
using a firehose,
the raging torrent
tears at their thin shirts.
Exposing shapes of breasts;
clinging wet cotton.
I feel their sex.
How they defied their captors—
livid, seething,
plotting revenge.

89

Define intimacy:
a moment fierce and close,
standing under a portico
in the middle of a warm summer rain,
grass soaks up the downpour.

There is no thing
as tender as acceptance.

I hid in my closet,
away from the gusting squalls of rage—
wished I could find that place
that was already there
inside me.

Decades
before I found a way
to take the next step.

90

A sable brush spreads
earthy ink on rice paper
the way peace soaks through
when I pray.

91

Yesterday
hot tears whistled through my bones.
I felt ten yards outside myself—
tried to come back to my body,
only to find
my gut tight,
buttock clenched,
a pinched low-back.

Then I thought—
my soul is loose
looking for a hilltop.

92

Living—
I think I do it satisfactorily,
getting past walls and doors.
But, I'm not sure.

Like a blind woman
I hear what's before me:
the shape of privets,
the obstacles—poles,
tricycles in my path.

It's the mist I can't hear,
the haze that doesn't echo.
The subtle.
Sighted or blind I mistake it.
When I show tenderness
I shy away from the pinch.
It takes me days to
find my way home.

93

To become a hero:
a girl born without legs is a mermaid,
without a voice is a composer,
without hearing is invisible.
Being angry means you're ablaze.

Still, our families shun us.
No one wants us to be imperfect.

I run on the sidewalk
in summer, smelling cut-grass,
fences thick with honeysuckle
the sounds of kids. Indecipherable hollering.

I jump on my bike and pedal without legs,
clothespins holding cards—clicking.
Pushing against ether—
a figurehead on the prow of a pirate ship.
I move without effort through waves.

94

Most nights are too long—at 3 a.m. I wish for mercy.
What are we anyway but mercury floating.

Animal gods bring me sleep if I'm lucky.
Cricket mouths open, red clicking in my skull.

I shake the shadows from my hair,
lie awake counting aches.

Tonight, I recognize the gift of my perseverance.
I saw her disembarking from the corner of my eye.

He stood on the dock waving at her to come ashore.
They've moved on, though not far from here.

95

The night is starless,
black-light posters, purple teeth, and
marijuana.

It's 1971.
Heavy, no sound, not even crickets –
vodka, dizzy air, thick molasses.
Sticks cut my bare bottom.
First Steve on top, then David breaking me open.
David, the boy on the school bus I slapped, hard.
Steve, the boy I had a schoolgirl crush on.

At fifty, I arrive at the scene,
approach my eighteen-year-old self,
"Let me handle this one for you," I say,
throwing the second one off. "Fuck you, leave her alone."
Before I take her home, my adult self walks
down the country road with Steve, whispers
how he'll pay for this for half his life.
His fingers crush his cigarette.

I tuck my drunk self into bed.
Don't worry, I'll take care of this.
She turns over like river stones.
Good, I came back to check on her—stupid girl.
You'll grow up to love yourself, I say.

96

There is a heaviness
in my chest;
a fishhook
tearing my gut.
Salty.

Do you know
crows can fashion and use a hook?
Turn life into art.

I remember once
catching my mother cry.
What's wrong?

Her shapely legs
glided the stairs.
Her eyes were red-rimmed.
I knew I couldn't make it better.
A hook pulling.

97

Dark circles around my hazel irises. I am recognizable in pieces: the rear-view mirror, a compact, a store window. Loving the shoes in need of repair, your long hair and your sideways laugh, your hand covering your mouth, the maps on the skin of my hands, lines that run over my breasts, up my neck.
Blessed be the ring around the fat full moon, my finger without
any rings. Blessed be the ripples descending into my groin and
the thoughts that repeat in my mind.
My father used to tremble as he stood in church, praying the *Our Father*.
Blessed be, blessed be our father who art in heaven.
By what grace did I meet you now?
When I was married, I would have pulled you out by your roots.
Today you have called me to your tractor, asked me to tag along.

98

Before the darkness settled in,
we planted corn, squash, kale, lettuce, carrots, beets, parsley.
The soft, red fruit tasted like tomatoes.
Peaches were with juice.
We picked the bounty before the blight and bugs.
Trees heavy with cherries, pears and apples.
We offered surplus to priests who danced by our house.
Large boned gods drank milk from our cows and showered us with grace.

99

We live in the darkness of time. Some say it's a moonlit night.
At 2 a.m. I see Buddha among succulents—on the deck—
the birds screech. Warning of unhinged predators, unfair destruction.
Sirens scream in the distance. I cross myself and say a prayer
for those traveling in ambulances. Crushed by cars
or the ones who mainline their veins with black tar. Euphoria I can't afford.
Tonight's moon has gone behind the clouds. Raccoons tear up the lawn.
The neighbors have turned off porch lights. I'm storing light in my chest.
Tomorrow the trash pick-up leaves a mess for me to clean and sweep.
Once, my grandmother pulled a full-length mirror on top of her,
it hit the bed post and shattered across her naked body.
I sent my shaken, sleepy parents from the room, gathered her up
whispering in her ear, 'it's okay, it's okay,' and picked up the shards.
Her fractured mind.
My only job is to give. Smile at the check-out worker.
Speak kindly to the delivery man. Look directly at a bully.
Show compassion for the crazy sisters.
Hiking a trail in the Montana mountains, I found myself leaping
before I even saw or heard the rattlesnake, the color of dirt and sage.
I felt its sexual writhing.
Somewhere a father screams, punches a hole in a wall.
A single mother raises her family. Children killed in war are lined up on an
embankment. Tumors riddle bones. Breasts lopped off. Memories wiped clean.
Bodies predict the ravages to come. The sick flock to sacred ground to repent.
Skin thin. Eyes hollow. Slacked jaws. Too late to pray or discover wings.
I'd like to transform the: "I've been wronged when someone cuts me off,"
or the: "I'm right no matter what the facts." I've been swimming gently
downstream—almost flying—when suddenly a tidal bore slaps me under.
I choke and tumble. Still, I don't fear death. I *yearn* to be One Thing.
Polish white stones as talismans, switch on lights in dark rooms,
fill my head with silence.   Teach the small gifts I've learned.

100

When it comes time
I will stand up and walk right out of my body.

I have loved being alive, giving birth to my son,
watching the moon rise, the stars chasing dog,

sitting in a rowboat on a lake at dusk, listening to the loons laugh,
kissing your lips, touching you, touching me.

I won't linger trying to remember those last words I wanted to say.
Let me tell them to you now: *I love you.*

This is not our last adventure,
no matter how much we want to know what's next,

Death is the best mystery we have.
I want to run into it with abandon,

just the way I let the wind whip my hair into knots
riding next to you in your red convertible.

BIOGRAPHY

Adele Slaughter is a poet and writer-director living in Los Angeles. Her short film, *Jealousy*, (2014) is based on her novel of the same name was seen in several film festivals. She received her M.F.A. in poetry from Columbia University. Slaughter's first book of poems, *What The Body Remembers* was published by Story Line Press in 1994 and is being reprinted by Red Hen Press. Her poems have appeared in Tupelo Press 30 in 30 Project, Poetry Bay, Everyday Genius, The Virginia Quarterly Review, Confrontation, Dryad and the Princeton Spectrum. She has taught at California State University Channel Islands, Glendale Community College, Pasadena City College and East Los Angeles Community College. Additionally, she has been a journalist covering personal health for USAToday.com. In 2004 she was awarded a national journalism prize for her coverage of multiple sclerosis. In 1993 the White House Commission on Presidential Scholars named her a Distinguished teacher. Slaughter and Jeff Kober co-wrote a non-fiction book entitled, Art That Pays: The Emerging Artist's Guide to Making a Living (NNAP, 2004). Recently, she began to throw pottery and hand-build clay into bowls and animals and painted spoons. She lives in Los Angeles where she teaches a writing workshop as well as assists her husband, Jeff Kober, who teaches meditation.

www.ingramcontent.com/pod-product-compliance
Lightning Source LLC
Chambersburg PA
CBHW072151200426
43209CB00052B/1116